I Know I Can!
Host A Party

ANTHEA DAVIDSON-JARRETT
Illustrated by
Aldana Penayo
Published by EDUCATE THE GLOBE,
London, UK, 2020.

ISBN: 978-1-913804-03-9

Copyright © 2020 Educate The Globe Limited. All rights reserved. No part of this book is to be reprinted, copied or stored in retrieval systems of any type, except by written permission from the author. Part of this book may, however, be used only in reference to support related documents or subjects.

I know I can do it!

Please can I help?

I want to do it all by myself!

Please can I try?

Can you show me how?

I'm not too small;

I am ready right now!

I'm having a party.

It's the end of school!

An all-white affair

and it's going to be cool!

Never hosted before.

I'm not sure what to do

but my daddy will help;

he's the party guru!

First thing's first!

I've got to send out the invites.

Not too many...

it's got to be just right!

Going to make my own

because creating is fun!

I think I will be generous

and add plus one!

Tell everybody

about the dress code;

look sharp in your white

or it's a no go!

By next week they need to

RSVP;

so I know how many

mouths I must feed.

Make sure that

my house is clean.

Tidy and neat;

crystal, pristine!

Decorate the place!

It's a celebration!

Congratulations

to the congregation!

Feel good sensation!

Our graduation

from education

is an elevation!

So now for the food.

Mummy's making Jollof.

I will make fruit punch;

make sure there's enough!

Daddy's making Waakye

and Red-Red.

It smells delicious!

He's a master chef.

Take care for allergies!

We don't want to see

drama at all.

No emergencies!

Set up the games.

Yes! Games galore!

It's a party after all;

I couldn't ask for more.

My brother will DJ;

he's good at that.

He makes bodies move

and that's a fact!

Food, drink and

lots of beautiful faces.

Great music and games;

it's so amazing!

It's so easy

to host a party

with a little help

from all the family!

www.ingramcontent.com/pod-product-compliance
Lightning Source LLC
Chambersburg PA
CBHW082053230426
43670CB00016B/2872